Art

LEVEL 5

/ue/aw/

DECODABLES BY jump!

Teaching Tips

Green Level 5

This book focuses on the phonemes **/ue/aw/**.

Before Reading

- Discuss the title. Ask readers what they think the book will be about. Have them briefly explain why.
- Ask readers to sort the words on page 3. Read the sounds and words together.

Read the Book

- Encourage readers to break down unfamiliar words into units of sound. Then, ask them to string the sounds together to create the words.
- Urge readers to point out when the focused phonics phonemes appear in the text.

After Reading

- Encourage children to reread the book independently or with a friend.
- Ask readers to name other words with /ue/ or /aw/ phonemes. On a separate sheet of paper, have them write the words out.

© 2024 Booklife Publishing
This edition is published by arrangement with Booklife Publishing.

North American adaptations © 2024 Jump!
5357 Penn Avenue South
Minneapolis, MN 55419
www.jumplibrary.com

Decodables by Jump! are published by Jump! Library.
All rights reserved. No part of this book may be reproduced in any form without written permission from the publisher.

Library of Congress Cataloging-in-Publication Data is available at www.loc.gov or upon request from the publisher.

ISBN: 979-8-88996-834-4 (hardcover)
ISBN: 979-8-88996-835-1 (paperback)
ISBN: 979-8-88996-836-8 (ebook)

Photo Credits

Images are courtesy of Shutterstock.com. With thanks to Getty Images, Thinkstock Photo and iStockphoto. Cover – New Africa. 4–5 – JeniFoto, Pressmaster. 6–7 – Krakenimages.com, Prostock-studio. 8–9 – Pranithan Chorruangsak, Yuliya Evstratenko. 10–11 – New Africa, Schweinepriester. 12–13 – JR-50, Tatevosian Yana. 14–15 – Krakenimages.com, phBodrova. 16 – Shutterstock.

Can you sort all the words on this page into two groups?

Clue

Claw

Words with
ue

Paw

Fuel

Straw

Words with
aw

Fawn

Blue

Do you draw, paint, or enjoy art? If you do, you are an artist!

You can make art with pens, paint, and glue. You can make art with lots of different things.

Get out all the things you need. You need a clear spot to make the art in.

If you do not have a clue how to start, do not panic. There is no need to rush.

What hues could you have in the art?
Blue is a cool hue. Red is a warm hue.

If the right hue is not there, you can mix the paint you have. You can mix a new hue.

You could make a self-portrait. A self-portrait is when a person draws or paints what they look like.

You do not have to make art of people. You could draw or paint an animal, such as a cat, dog, or hawk.

You could go out to draw or paint. Lots of people paint their town at dawn or paint a sunset.

You can make art on the street. You can clean it off in a bit or wait for the rain.

You can collect things from outside and make them into a statue.

If you think art is fun, you could do it as a job when you are big!

Sound out each word. Does it have a /ue/ or /aw/ sound?

tissue

saw

clue

lawn